Rhythm of Love

Rhythm of Devotion

Mason D. Powell and Alexander Hildebrand

Published by Archippus, 2024.

While every precaution has been taken in the preparation of this book, the publisher assumes no responsibility for errors or omissions, or for damages resulting from the use of the information contained herein.

RHYTHM OF LOVE

First edition. November 10, 2024.

ISBN: 979-8227156037

Written by Mason D. Powell and Alexander Hildebrand.

Table of Contents

Introduction...1

Love Consumes Our Focus...7

Love Reveals Character 10

Love Burns Like Fire 13

Sex is Intimate Knowing...16

Sex is Celebration 19

Sex is Life Giving 22

Commitment is More Than a Feeling 25

Commitment is Exclusive 28

Commitment is Painful When Broken.........................31

Problems Will Arise 34

Problems Can Break Boundaries.................................37

Problems Can Lead To Intimacy.................................40

Our Bodies Are Beautiful...43

Our Relationship is Beautiful.....................................46

Our Innate Worth is Beautiful....................................49

Free Book..52

About the Authors...53

"To Emily, my bride."

—Alex

"And to Jodi, my love."

—Mason

Note from the Authors

Thank you for checking out our Song of Songs devotional!

We hope that as you engage with this devotional that you will develop a greater connection to God and His Word. This little devotional was first released in Mason's church to accompany a sermon series he delivered walking through Song of Songs. If you would like to watch the sermon videos that go along with each week's reading, you can find it by searching for the series, A Legendary Love, over at www.thebluff.church[1].

It is important to note that this book is not a commentary on the text. No devotional ever is. Nor is it a replacement for soul-searching study and meditation of Scripture. But we hope that this short devotional encourages readers to question what it means to be part of a gospel centered marriage following Jesus.

You may find, as you read this book, or any of our devotional pieces, that some themes repeat themselves. You might even find that some of the reflection questions and challenges sound repetitive. This is not a bad thing, but done a bit intentionally. Repetition is how we learn and grow. Repetitive questions and content force us to give them answers worthy of our time and attention. Because some New Testament writing operates like this, we have tried to incorporate those same principles in these devotionals.

---

1. http://www.thebluff.church

We would ask that if you enjoy this book that you would consider leaving a review online wherever you got this book. Your review means everything to us, as it helps give this book more exposure to encourage more couples out there.

And if you find this devotional uplifting, the highest honor you can give us would be to share it with a friend to encourage them after you are done.

Again, thanks for reading this short devotional of ours.

Happy reading!

Mason D. Powell and Alexander Hildebrand

Introduction

Love, and its culmination in an intimate and faithful marriage, captures the attention of humanity more than any other topic. Countless books, poems, songs, and movies have been written about love. From the beginning of time, mankind has been obsessed with this topic. We are drawn to love. We long to be loved. We seek it, and fight for it, and are filled with great sadness when we lose it.

Love is powerful. It is a force that can heal and a force that can wound. Love deserves high praise when seen in a thriving state of health, but if treated improperly, it can cause tremendous pain. The powerful nature by which love captures the heart of humanity points us to something far greater than ourselves. Love is a force which reflects the Creator who placed it within our hearts.

John succinctly writes, *"Beloved, let's love one another; for love is from God, and everyone who loves has been born of God and knows God. The one who does not love does not know God, because God is love."* (1 John 4:7-8, NASB)

If we want to know what true love looks like, we need to know who God is. Love comes from God. Love is found in God. Since God is love, and God is beyond our comprehension in countless ways, there is no exhaustive amount that can be said about love. Authors and artists have been writing about love for thousands of years, and it does not appear that they will be slowing down any time soon.

As such, this small devotional is but a drop in an ocean of material that seeks to do one thing: to move us deeper into being people of love. This devotional does not contain any new developments in the discovery of love or newfound approaches. Rather, this devotional is built on the truths which the Scriptures have proclaimed for thousands of years:

- God is love.

- God loved us before we ever knew Him.

- God poured out His love for us through the life and death of Christ Jesus.

- If we want to follow Christ, we must love as He loved.

- If we want to love as Christ loved, we must know Him well.

God designed romantic love as extension and reflection of His love for us. The Song of Songs is a Scripture focused on celebrating this gift from God. Our hope is that as you work through this devotional, you would grow in your knowledge of God, your knowledge of yourselves, and your knowledge of your betrothed. If we want to grow in our love, we must grow in our knowing.

Our prayer is that this material will help you foster greater awe for the love of Christ, and a greater sense of how that love plays out in the most intimate human relationship you can have.

How To Use This Devotional

This devotional focuses on five topics: Love, Sex, Commitment, Problems, and Beauty. Each topic has three entries which are intended to be read over the course of one week. Each entry should be read on its own day – try not to work through multiple entries in the same day. If you follow this schedule, it will take you five weeks to work through the entire devotional.

Each entry has the following sections for you to read and follow:

• Opening Prayer – This is a written prayer designed to help the reader focus on God and His Word.

• Texts to Read – These are the passages of Scripture for you to read and meditate on.

• Main Takeaway (Melody) – This is the "main point" that we would like you to dwell on when applying the Scriptures to your own life.

• Challenge (Harmony) – This is an action step for you and your betrothed to set aside time and discuss certain topics.

• Look to Christ (Rhythm) – This is a description of how the Scriptures and applications are made evident in the person of Jesus.

• Closing Prayer – This is a written prayer designed to lead the reader in coming before God in humility to be shaped and formed in the likeness of Christ.

Melody/Harmony/Rhythm Description:

Because the Song of Songs is Hebrew poetry meant to be sung in a public gathering, we arranged the daily material in this devotional to follow a more rhythmic style found in music. Every song has three foundational components: Melody, Harmony, and Rhythm. Melody is the "lead tune" of the song. It's typically what you would sing or whistle. Harmony is when different notes come together to form a unique sound made only possible by the combination of these different notes. Rhythm is the timing of a song and gives the music a tempo and feel.

All three components work together to create beautiful pieces of music. Like the components in music, we structured this devotional with three parts for each day. The Melody of each day examines wisdom seen within the Song of Songs for couples. The Harmony is a practical application on how you and your spouse can practice the wisdom discussed. The Rhythm draws our attention back to Jesus to see how the first two sections derive themselves from the source of God's love.

Engaging With Your Spouse

For those who are married, we greatly encourage you to work through this devotional with your spouse. Here is some practical advice on how to utilize this devotional together:

1. Decide to read the devotional entries together or separate. It is perfectly fine for you and your spouse to read the entries separately as long as you commit to discussing each entry together at a later time. Reading

together will help foster a sense of togetherness as you come to the Scriptures, but reading individually can give you time to dwell and ponder the text before you discuss it. Discuss with your spouse the best strategy needed for your relationship.

2. Put it on your calendar to read and discuss the devotions. There are 3 entries for each of the major themes. You can rush through the entire booklet in 15 days straight, but we recommend spending a week on each theme. This slower pace will give you time to better reflect on each topic and the ways it speaks to your marriage. It can be easy to get distracted or become busy. We highly recommend that you schedule intentional time upfront to work through the devotional.

3. When discussing the texts and prompts, do not use accusatory language. This can be easy to do, and would be the opposite of beneficial. This booklet is not designed to show you all the ways that your spouse is wrong. This devotional is designed to bring you and your spouse into greater intimacy. Curiosity is always better than aggression and accusation in any marital discussion. We should always be quick to listen and slow to speak. Therefore, focus on evaluating yourself instead of your spouse. Listen to your spouse intently and seek to understand them. Approach this devotional not with the intent of figuring out how to fix your spouse, but to see how you can grow in your love of God and your spouse.

For Those Not Married

The Song of Songs has value for everyone, not just those who are married. For those seeking a future marriage, approach this devotion as educational for preparation. Let the wisdom and passion of the Song of Songs shape and form your perception about what a healthy, loving marriage looks like.

Whether you are seeking to be married later in your life or not, keep in mind that many of the principles found in the Song of Songs can apply to non-sexual relationships through the use of metaphor. The marriage relationship is one of the key metaphors used to describe the relationship between God and Israel in the Old Testament and Christ and the Church in the New Testament. As such, the passionate sexual love of the bride and the groom in the Song of Songs has wisdom for us as we understand our relationship with Christ and even our platonic relationships with one another.

When it comes to the "Challenge" section of each entry, we encourage you to do two things: First, look for the general underlying concept behind the challenge which can be applied to any kind of relationship. Second, ask yourself where you have seen positive examples of the challenge in married couples around you. This may be a bit difficult depending on the section (mainly the entries discussing sex), but the principles of love found in Song of Songs can be applied to our relationship with our Savior for He is our groom.

Love Consumes Our Focus

Opening Prayer

Jesus,

We thank you for the beauty of your Word and the wisdom it has for us today. Please open our ears to hear you, our eyes to see your beauty, our hearts to receive your love, and our hands to be of service to you.

Amen.

Texts To Read

Song of Songs 4:9-10

Matthew 4:23-25

Main Takeaway (Melody)

Love, especially youthful love, does this funny thing to us. As one develops an initial attraction to another, it is easy to become "love-drunk." Our minds often drift into daydreams of our beloved, and some may simply repeat the name of their crush, as the name alone brings delight. As you read through the Song of Songs, you see that the bride and groom in the poem are "love-drunk" for each other. All they can think about is the other individual and how much they love them.

What we love is what our mind focuses on.

Whether it is a person, a hobby, or a goal, our love dictates our attention. Since love is such a powerful force, let us be careful what we set our heart's desire on. Likewise, that which we give our attention can cultivate, or even reawaken, the feeling of love. Love and attention are interconnected forces we must be mindful of. As such, let us examine where

Challenge (Harmony)

Discuss with your spouse how much attention you each are giving toward the relationship, your feelings on that amount, and where you would like it to be.

Look to Christ (Rhythm)

Jesus was attentive to those He loved. He was locked in on his mission to help the broken, heal the sick, feed the hungry, teach the longing, and proclaim the good news of the Kingdom of God. His focus was clearly on the surrounding people, to be the source of light in their darkness and to share with them love. Jesus is still going about doing this work today. Jesus loves you and focuses on you. How can you daily give your attention to Christ? How does the continual, focused love of Christ encourage you to daily love your spouse?

Closing Prayer

Jesus,

Our minds are fickle things. We so easily lose focus or fixate on that which does not warrant our attention. At a time where everything is fighting for our focus, spark a new love for You and a desire for those You have put before us. Help us examine the feelings that draw our attention, and help us make the conscious decision to fix our attention on that which we know is worthy of our love, but at the moment, we may not feel. Thank You for Your continued faithfulness to us, which is born out of Your love for us.

Amen.

Love Reveals Character

Opening Prayer

Jesus,

We thank you for the beauty of your Word and the wisdom it has for us today. Please open our ears to hear you, our eyes to see your beauty, our hearts to receive your love, and our hands to be of service to you.

Amen.

Texts To Read

Song of Songs 1:3

John 1:1-14

Main Takeaway (Melody)

This poem begins with the bride expressing her attraction and desire for intimacy with the groom. What is interesting to note is that the bride was first attracted to the groom's character. His good name is described as oil being poured out. His character mattered more than anything else.

When love is first blossoming, there are many reasons why we might be attracted to another, but not all those reasons may be good.

Throughout the Bible, character is regarded as having a greater importance than any other attractive quality. Beauty, money, and all other things eventually diminish and fade. When everything else has fallen away, what remains is one's character. A love that is rich will celebrate the character of their partner. They elevate their beloved's character above all other things. They proclaim it to others and praise their partner when they see good qualities in them in order to help their partner's greater character continue to rise to the surface.

Challenge (Harmony)

Discuss what qualities first attracted you to your spouse and what qualities you appreciate in them now.

Christ (Rhythm)

Before Jesus ever took the cross, it was His character that attracted people, and it was His character that eventually led Him to the cross. In the Gospel of John, John wants us to see Jesus, to see His character, to see in Him that God has sought to dwell among us so that we might see His grace and love. The character of Jesus shows us how much God wants to be where we are and us where He is. The character of Jesus shows us the grace that God has for us. The character of Jesus shows us the extraordinary love that God has for us. Being in a relationship with God is not about getting to heaven, it is about being consumed with awe and love for the character of Jesus, and seeking to embody that character in our own lives.

Closing Prayer

Jesus,

We love You, not merely because of what You have done for us, but because of who You are. Your character inspires us and reminds us it is character more than anything else that drew us toward our spouse. Teach us to celebrate their excellent character, and help us embody more of Your character in our marriage.

Amen.

Love Burns Like Fire

Opening Prayer

Jesus,

We thank you for the beauty of your Word and the wisdom it has for us today. Please open our ears to hear you, our eyes to see your beauty, our hearts to receive your love, and our hands to be of service to you.

Amen.

Texts To Read

Song of Songs 8:6-7

Hebrews 12:29

Main Takeaway (Melody)

The ending of the Song summarizes the main takeaway of the entire poem. Here the bride gives commentary on what love is and how it has played into her life. She describes love as a consuming fire that washed over her like a flood. Anyone who has fallen in love knows the feeling well, and they know it burns like fire. They also know the delight, joy, and agony that is involved.

Fire is wild.

When maintained and properly cared for, fire sustains life and provides security. Fire provides light and warmth, necessary for our survival. Just as fire is necessary for our survival, it can also bring about disaster. If it is not controlled and managed, fire can cause great harm and destruction. When neglected, fire can rage or easily be snuffed out. Love can be the same way. Bringing forth love can be a gradual process, but if neglected, it has the potential to cause significant harm or fade away. But when love is nourished and cared for, it provides such rich blessings for those who share it together. The bride and groom experienced this, and all those who are married ought to take it into account. How are we working to nourish love in our relationship to receive its rich blessings for us?

Challenge (Harmony)

Discuss with your spouse what things your partner does that make you feel the most loved and close to them. How can you protect, nurture, and maintain your love with one another?

Look to Christ (Rhythm)

Throughout the Bible, God displays His presence and power as a fire. Sometimes this fire is a sign of God's faithfulness such as the example of Elijah's famous contest. Other times it is a sign of God's security and presence like the burning bush or His guidance through the wilderness. At other time's fire is used to display God's justice and protection for His creation. God's love is holy, passionate, and powerful, something that should not be approached carelessly.

Christ's life, death, and resurrection has enabled us to be in the presence of God's fiery love. The author of Hebrews describes God as a consuming fire, but He is not a fire we should run away from! For earlier in his sermon, the author of Hebrews declares that since Jesus is our great high priest, we can boldly approach the throne of God (Heb. 4:14-16). Christ's perfect love has enabled us experience the passionate, wild love of God in perfect security.

Closing Prayer

Jesus,

Thank You for Your love that burns like fire. Thank You for how You teach us to share that love with others. Guide us to love in such a way that we bring forth rich blessings in our most vital relationships, just as You have done for us.

Amen.

Sex is Intimate Knowing

Opening Prayer

Jesus,

We thank you for the beauty of your Word and the wisdom it has for us today. Please open our ears to hear you, our eyes to see your beauty, our hearts to receive your love, and our hands to be of service to you.

Amen.

Texts To Read

Song of Songs 5:9-6:3

Genesis. 2:24-25, 4:1

Philippians 3:7-11

Main Takeaway (Melody)

Throughout the Song of Songs, the bride and groom describe each other's bodies with great personal detail and imaginative imagery. While the descriptions might sound strange to us, the intimacy within it is easy to grasp, and represents a deep knowing that the two have for each other. In Genesis 4:1, the author uses the phrase "to know" in order to describe sexual intercourse. While other words could have been used to describe this act, this wordplay is intentional and frequently used in a positive light within Scripture.

By using the phrase "to know," the biblical authors describe sex as being incredibly intimate.

A husband and wife know one another by being intimate with one another, which includes sexual intimacy. God designed the physical act of sex for this reason, that the two would fully embrace one other and become one flesh. This is why sex is such a unique experience; human bodies cannot get any closer in any other way! A healthy marriage is one in which the husband and wife know one another through intimacy with one another - physically, emotionally, sexually, and spiritually. Intimacy cannot exist without truly knowing someone. Knowing someone cannot happen unless we spend time with them. Married couples have the opportunity to experience an incredibly intimate moment with one another which fosters a unique relational unity.

Challenge (Harmony)

Discuss with your partner what you feel each of you is needing from the other in order to feel fully known.

Look to Christ (Rhythm)

Jesus knows us better than we know ourselves. He knows our needs, our wants, our thoughts, and everything else there is to know about us. Jesus knows us, and He wants us to know Him. We will not fully know Jesus in a single day, just like we will not fully know our spouse in a single day. Knowing Jesus is a lifelong pursuit. How are you intentionally seeking to know Jesus? How are you being vulnerable with Jesus? How does the intimate love of Jesus shape and form your love for your spouse?

Closing Prayer

Jesus,

Thank You for knowing us. You made us and know our hearts. You know us better than we know ourselves. Give us a passion to know You greater and teach us how to live with that same passion toward our spouses. May they come to see and believe that we truly want to know them as deeply as we can in every way imaginable, as we in time share that passion toward You.

Amen.

Sex is Celebration

Opening Prayer

Jesus,

We thank you for the beauty of your Word and the wisdom it has for us today. Please open our ears to hear you, our eyes to see your beauty, our hearts to receive your love, and our hands to be of service to you.

Amen.

Texts To Read

Song of Songs 4:1-5:1

Psalm 37:4

Main Takeaway (Melody)

There is a difference between good sex and great sex, and the pair of lovers in this song have discovered the difference. It is not about form or technique or frequency of sex, rather the difference has been found in how the two have shared a deep emotional vulnerability with each other. They have opened their hearts to each other. They have shared expressions of love.

Their delight was first to be in each other's presence, to have an intimate knowledge of the other, before delighting in the bedroom.

Because of that open emotional vulnerability, the two finally come together and discover a delight that each describes to be like tasting sweet fruit, honey, and wine. They have come to fully desire the other, and in that mutual desire, they discovered sex that was more than just physical but also emotional and spiritual. This was all because the two were open and honest with each other, sharing their desires and not afraid to be open about their vulnerabilities. Sex was not the goal of the relationship, but a celebration of their love for one another.

Challenge (Harmony)

Discuss your emotional openness with your partner. Is it easy for you to be vulnerable or difficult? What can you do to make it easier for your partner to be more emotionally vulnerable?

Look to Christ (Rhythm)

God wants to be the delight of our hearts more than anything else. Often, we look to God merely when we are in need or see Him only as our rescuer from trouble. But we should ask ourselves, would we be pleased if people only came to us when they needed something from us? Christian maturity involves coming to a place where our love for God is for Him before what He can do for us. God wants us to delight ourselves in Him, to be thrilled simply to be with Him, and to know that we can be vulnerable with Him. We can share our hearts, our dreams, our desires, and our concerns with Him, even if they are about having a relationship with Him. It is something God desires in a relationship with us, why He came to dwell with us, and what an intimate relationship with Him looks like.

Closing Prayer

Jesus,

We see in Your words how clearly you delight in us and desire to be with us. You made us feel at home in Your presence, to feel safe and seen and loved. As we discover the delight in being with You, may that spill over into our most intimate of relationships. Teach us to delight in our loved ones by softening our hearts to be emotionally vulnerable with each other and opening ourselves up to love.

Amen.

Sex is Life Giving

Opening Prayer

Jesus,

We thank you for the beauty of your Word and the wisdom it has for us today. Please open our ears to hear you, our eyes to see your beauty, our hearts to receive your love, and our hands to be of service to you.

Amen.

Texts To Read

Song of Songs 8:1-7

John 13:34-35

Main Takeaway (Melody)

Would you bring up your parents while trying to be romantic with your spouse? Song of Songs 8:1-7 comes across as strange to us today because it does precisely that. In our culture, the thought of family is often repulsive during feelings of romance and intimacy. However, our culture did not write the Bible. The Scriptures originated from a culture that prioritized family. The individuality and separation that we see as normal would come across as quite confusing to those in these family-centric cultures. While God designed sexual gintimacy to be kept solely between a husband and wife, He also designed sexual intimacy to have a wide-reaching impact.

A husband's and wife's sexual intimacy, or lack thereof, will affect the lives of their family members.

Most obviously, sexual intimacy allows for the creation and addition of more people into the family. This is such a wonderful mystery! It is through the union of a husband and wife that a child comes to be. But even as a child grows, their parents' sexual intimacy will continue to affect them. If sexual intimacy plays a role in making a husband and wife one flesh, then that unity will carry over into how those spouses work together to raise their children. Children can perceive, either consciously or subconsciously, if their parents are unified or not. Sexual intimacy has the power to create life, and it has the power to bring life into our family relationships day after day through cultivating unity between spouses.

Challenge (Harmony)

Discuss with your spouse how you feel about your sexual intimacy as a couple, how it blesses you or if there are any pains that need to be discussed and what can be done to make intimacy more life-giving to both partners.

Look to Christ (Rhythm)

The more we love Christ, the more we will love one another. The Bible is abundantly clear that our relationship with Jesus will also drastically affect the relationship that we have with others. Likewise, the relationship you have with your spouse will affect the relationship you have with your children and other family members. As you seek to love Christ more, seek to love your spouse more. And as you seek to love your spouse more, seek to love your family more.

Closing Prayer

Jesus,

What a great mystery You have made that love is always a community thing. The more we love You, the more that shapes our love toward others. When we receive love, it gives us life, and we share that life with others by our love expressed toward them. Give us a greater awe and understanding of Your love, and give us a greater urgency to share that love out with others. For You are our life and we seek to share Your life out in this world, especially in our homes.

Amen.

Commitment is More Than a Feeling

Opening Prayer

Jesus,

We thank you for the beauty of your Word and the wisdom it has for us today. Please open our ears to hear you, our eyes to see your beauty, our hearts to receive your love, and our hands to be of service to you.

Amen.

Texts To Read

Song of Songs 2:16

John 4:1-42

Main Takeaway (Melody)

The Song of Songs expresses a lot of feelings between the bride and groom regarding their love. Love certainly wraps itself up with a lot of feelings, but love is more than a feeling. Love is a choice and with that choice is the vow to be committed to each other. Everyone has certain needs to feel loved, and in a thriving relationship, partners commit to fostering that love by knowing and fulfilling those needs. To say you belong to someone and that they belong to you requires each spouse to unveil their needs before one another. Each spouse must trust each other to take responsibility in the pursuit to satisfy the needs of the other. Everyone needs six aspects to feel loved:

- To feel Safe,

- To feel Seen,

- To feel Heard,

- To feel Appreciated,

- To feel Validated,

- To feel Respected.

All six of these needs combine to make someone feel loved. The degree to which everyone needs these requirements varies from male and female, and certainly from person to person. Some people place a higher importance on knowing they are appreciated than on feeling heard. Others need to feel like they are safe with their partner more than they need to feel respected by their partner. A lifetime of being committed to your partner means continually seeking to know and satisfy their needs over your own.

Challenge (Harmony)

Discuss what you feel you need most right now in your relationship from the six essentials to love mentioned above.

Look to Christ (Rhythm)

Throughout the Gospels, people approach Jesus with a problem, or he approaches them to address a problem. They need something, or they think they need one thing when they actually need something else. Again and again, Jesus proves he knows what those around Him need, and is eager to provide that need. The famous story of John 4 of Jesus meeting the Samaritan woman at the well embodies this truth. Jesus knew her story, what she needed, and the many pains she had experienced searching for what she needed. He didn't shame or judge her but offered her instead the very thing she had spent her entire life searching for, and he did it with extraordinary gentleness and love. Read the Gospels carefully and you will see how Jesus treats people with love displayed in all six of the pillars to love, showing His commitment to us. Jesus knows our needs, and He speaks on that often, and talks about His eagerness to give us what we need in this life. He is committed to us, and He promises that will never change.

Closing Prayer

Jesus,

Thank You for Your example of what it means to be committed to a relationship with us. You sacrifice for us, showing You both know our needs and desire to fulfill our needs. Teach us to love in commitment toward those You have called us to love. Teach us what it means to be committed to our spouse as we see Your commitment to Your church.

Amen.

Commitment is Exclusive

Opening Prayer

Jesus,

We thank you for the beauty of your Word and the wisdom it has for us today. Please open our ears to hear you, our eyes to see your beauty, our hearts to receive your love, and our hands to be of service to you.

Amen.

Texts To Read

Song of Songs 8:11-12

Matthew 23:37

Main Takeaway (Melody)

The ending of the song finds the lovers faced with a challenge. The song mentions Solomon, who had many vineyards and servants, and compares him to the couple in this song. Some see this ending as Solomon as a villain, seeing the intimacy of the two lovers and wanting to buy that for himself. He comes in with an impressive amount of wealth and possessions and makes a proposition to the bride for her to leave her groom and be part of his harem. Others see Solomon as the groom late in his years with many wives and the wife expressing her lament that she is no longer his sole lover. He was not exclusive to her. The second reading comes with heartache, but the first shows an inspiring message that our lovers see their relationship so valuable that they don't want to share it or give it away for anything else.

Their commitment to each other, above all else, has resulted in a joyful marriage.

However you interpret these verses, they either impart an inspiring message of the joy commitment can bring in the face of obstacles and trials, or a lesson of woe and heartache when commitment is broken for lesser things. Both viewpoints speak of the importance of an exclusive commitment in love.

Challenge (Harmony)

Share with your spouse something exclusive with them. Ideas might include feelings, dreams, insecurities, pains, hopes, desires.

Look to Christ (Rhythm)

From the moment that God established a covenant with His people, it was exclusive. He was their God, and they were His people. God would not put up with outsiders encroaching on His territory. He was jealous of the heart of His people, and He made that plainly known. The people knew what type of relationship God wanted with them. Unfortunately, they did not want the same. Again and again, it was the people, not God, who did not keep this covenant exclusive—yet that didn't change God's heart. He wanted to be the only arms that wrapped around His people. He wanted them to feel safe in His embrace.

So again and again, God pursued His people. Jesus carries this forward, again and again crying out for His people to repent and return to God, only to find that their relationship with God was no longer exclusive. God desires an exclusive relationship with us. He wants to be our God that we commit to, and He wants that commitment to inspire godly character and action in every area of our lives.

Closing Prayer

Jesus,

Thank You for always being more committed to us than we are to You. You are faithful when we are fickle and prone to wander. Yet You still declare Your love for us and remain constant in Your commitment to us. Guide us back into sharing that exclusive commitment with You, and may it inspire us to do the same in our most vital of relationships.

Amen.

Commitment is Painful When Broken

Opening Prayer

Jesus,

We thank you for the beauty of your Word and the wisdom it has for us today. Please open our ears to hear you, our eyes to see your beauty, our hearts to receive your love, and our hands to be of service to you.

Amen.

Texts To Read

Song of Songs 3:1-5

John 21:15-19

Main Takeaway (Melody)

There are two moments in the Song of Songs in which the bride experiences great turmoil. The first moment is in chapter three, where the bride expresses distress and painful longing when she cannot be with her beloved. The second moment is during a conflict between the bride and her husband in chapter five.

When we become attached to someone, moments of detachment from that person become incredibly painful.

Whether it is a physical separation, a relational conflict, or even covenant betrayal, the more we love someone, the more we will feel pain when commitment is broken. The bride knows this experience well and cautions women younger than her to not awaken love until the time is right. Love requires maturity and commitment. If maturity and commitment are absent, the lovers will experience great pain.

Challenge (Harmony)

Be honest with each other, with lots of grace and mercy, of the pains caused by failure to be committed. Then pray over each other and those situations.

Look to Christ (Rhythm)

Jesus promises to never leave us or forsake us. Christ is the one constant in our life in which we can fully place our trust with no fear of betrayal or separation. And this is true even considering our own constant betrayal to him. When Jesus was arrested, Peter did not demonstrate true commitment to Jesus. We can read the account in each of the Gospels and feel the pain both Peter and Jesus feel in this. Yet Jesus still welcomes Peter back, forgives him for the pain of betrayal, and shows him love. And Jesus does the same for us day after day. Even when we sin against God, God continually reminds us He loves us and does not abandon us.

Closing Prayer

Jesus,

Forgive us. We know we have caused You great pain. You have committed yourself to us, knowing fully well that we have hurt You and will continue to hurt You because of our lack of commitment. Yet You remain. You give out grace and mercy and love. Teach us to do the same for others—especially our spouses—when they hurt us. When those times come, teach us to be as gracious, patient, merciful, and forgiving as You have been to us.

Amen.

Problems Will Arise

Opening Prayer

Jesus,

We thank you for the beauty of your Word and the wisdom it has for us today. Please open our ears to hear you, our eyes to see your beauty, our hearts to receive your love, and our hands to be of service to you.

Amen.

Texts To Read

Song of Songs 5:2-8

Ephesians 2:13-15

Main Takeaway (Melody)

The middle section of the Song of Songs curiously depicts a conflict between the groom and the bride. While most of the song consists of the couple swooning over each other, this middle section intentionally depicts a conflict. We don't know what caused this problem, or even what it is exactly, but we can clearly see its effects on the relationship. The groom wants to be with the bride, but the bride initially refuses. Then, after changing her mind, the bride goes to receive the groom, only to find that he has left!

For one reason or another, marriages will experience problems.

Problems can create some kind of separation, whether it be physical, emotional, sexual, or in some other fashion. It is important to recognize that problems within a marriage are to be expected, and that problems not handled properly naturally produce separation—which is the opposite of God's intention for the marriage relationship. However, problems can be a catalyst for future intimacy when a couple learns how to fight fair and plan for how they will handle problems.

Challenge (Harmony)

Create some guidelines for how you will address problems with your spouse. When problems arise, how should you communicate? What language must be avoided? How can you pause and reset for healthy communication?

Look to Christ (Rhythm)

While our sin against God created separation in the garden of Eden, Christ intentionally eliminated that separation by making himself close to us. God has never been the guilty party between us. We always have been the ones at fault. We all have sinned against God, creating a problem and a following separation. But God did not settle for that separation. He could have, and none would have judged Him. Yet because of His great love for us, God did not give up on us. He had every intention of making a means of reconciliation for us. God sent Jesus to solve our great conflict with him. Jesus is called Emmanuel, which means "God with us." If God's response to our sin is to make Himself close to us, how should we respond to others when problems arise?

Closing Prayer

Jesus,

Thank You for not giving up on us. You had every right to because what we have done again and again to You was wrong. But You do not walk away from us. Your great love is a constant comfort and a constant guide through the conflicts in our life. Teach us to make peace like You did for us.

Amen.

Problems Can Break Boundaries

Opening Prayer

Jesus,

We thank you for the beauty of your Word and the wisdom it has for us today. Please open our ears to hear you, our eyes to see your beauty, our hearts to receive your love, and our hands to be of service to you.

Amen.

Texts To Read

Song of Songs 2:15

Romans 6:20-23

Main Takeaway (Melody)

The groom and bride in the Song describe their relationship often like a garden or vineyard. It was a place of life, but they understood that this life only thrived when carefully maintained. That maintenance included keeping unhealthy things out, like foxes. They used symbolic language to address the fact that for their relationship to thrive, some things needed to be kept outside the boundaries of their relationship. Every relationship, especially a marriage relationship, requires healthy boundaries. Some things need to be left out of the relationship in order for things to remain healthy.

It is a complicated matter when two become one.

Each partner comes into the relationship with desires and expectations and assumptions. Then there is family history and relationships with others to be considered. Boundaries are essential for navigating this space and preserving what is healthy. Setting and enforcing boundaries, especially in a marriage, might not seem like the most loving thing to do. In the short run, it might cause more conflicts when we enforce those boundaries. But boundaries help prevent long-term harm, even if they require temporary hurts, so that the relationship can thrive. Therefore, one effective approach to handling problems and avoiding them in the future is to establish clear guidelines for what is healthy and unhealthy in a marriage.

Challenge (Harmony)

Discuss what "foxes" need to stay out of your relationship for things to be healthy between you and your spouse.

Look to Christ (Rhythm)

From the beginning, God has understood that boundaries are good and necessary. It was God's love and wisdom which brought forth the command to Adam and Eve to not to eat from the forbidden tree. In the same manner, it was loving and wise for God to give the Israelites the Ten Commandments. The same can be said for why there was a restriction on who could enter the temple, why touching the Ark of the Covenant was forbidden, why sacrifices were necessary, and why God asks his people to do certain things and avoid other things. God wants us to be in a thriving relationship with Him, one that is full of life. But our self-destructive nature calls for restraint. It calls for "foxes" to be removed and boundaries to be submitted to. Because God is holy and we are not, it is God who sets the boundaries on how we can be with Him. Therefore, sin deeply hurts God because it involves a step across a boundary God has said is necessary for a thriving relationship with Him. Through faith in the perfection of Christ, restoration happens, and through His faithfulness we can find a new thriving in this relationship with God.

Closing Prayer

Jesus,

Thank You for Your boundaries. They give us clarity and they give us a safe space. You give boundaries because You intend to keep us from harm, and You give them because You seek for our thriving. May we learn to see them the same in our relationships, and may we set and enforce them so that our earthly relationships might be the spaces where we can effectively show Your love to the world.

Amen.

Problems Can Lead To Intimacy

Opening Prayer

Jesus,

We thank you for the beauty of your Word and the wisdom it has for us today. Please open our ears to hear you, our eyes to see your beauty, our hearts to receive your love, and our hands to be of service to you.

Amen.

Texts To Read

Song of Songs 7:10

Luke 7:36-50

Main Takeaway (Melody)

When the bride and groom have worked through their issues and conflict, the result is not a mere restoration of the relationship, but a deepening of it. The matter which threatened them, when handled appropriately, has resulted in the two by the end of the song having a deeper bond with one another. Their love is no longer built on hormones but has been tested by fire and pruned to become something more glorious and abundant. They are more than the people attracted to each other. They are the people who have chosen each other, especially in the face of conflict.

When the conflict threatened to wound and tear them apart, they remained steadfast in their decision to still choose the other.

Now bride and groom reap the rewards for that continual faithfulness. Conflict can be healthy in a marriage, and any relationship, when handled properly. In the middle of the conflict, it might not feel that things can get better, but when perseverance, honesty, and humility are applied to a relationship, the outcome can produce a greater love than what was before.

Challenge (Harmony)

Pray together for the continual growth and maturity of your marriage.

Look to Christ (Rhythm)

Jesus pointed to this Main Takeaway being true in our relationship with God when it came to forgiveness, as seen in the story in Luke 7. The woman was a great sinner, but discovering a God who offered her a greater forgiveness she fell more in love. This isn't an encouragement to sin more to grow our love more, only that we should find ourselves in greater awe and greater love the more we realize just how grave our conflict with God was and how mighty His grace and mercy for us is.

Closing Prayer

Jesus,

Our conflict with You was far greater than we could ever hope to imagine or understand. Yet You offer forgiveness and never give up on us. The more we see that, the greater our love for You. Help us to treat our relational conflicts the same way, as an opportunity that through this pruning something greater might take birth than what was before.

Amen.

Our Bodies Are Beautiful

Opening Prayer

Jesus,

We thank you for the beauty of your Word and the wisdom it has for us today. Please open our ears to hear you, our eyes to see your beauty, our hearts to receive your love, and our hands to be of service to you.

Amen.

Texts To Read

Song of Songs 1:15-2:2

1 Corinthians 12:12-31

Main Takeaway (Melody)

It is quite clear that the bride and the groom within the poem of Song of Songs see each other as beautiful and attractive. Looks certainly are not everything in a relationship, and we should not elevate them as a priority, but that does not mean we should regard them as evil or nonexistent. The couple revels in each other's physical beauty, not of their own beauty but in how they find their partner attractive. Their bodies are not something to be avoided or ignored. The physical bodies of their lover are something to be seen and delighted in. The same is true for the presence they offer each other.

God made human beings to be beautiful.

Our beauty is a good gift from God, a gift which should not be ignored. Each of our bodies are unique and loved by our Creator, so we should take great care to see the uniqueness of our spouse's body and love it! This love and recognition are something to be delightful, but not selfish. Rejoicing in the beauty of your spouse's body should be seen as a gift from God, not an idol to replace Him. Likewise, we must not fall into the trap of comparing our spouse's beauty to the beauty of others. Instead, let us humbly thank God for our body and for the body of our spouse. Let us daily see the gifts He has given us and enjoy them as He intended.

Challenge (Harmony)

Share three physical attributes you find attractive in your spouse.

Look to Christ (Rhythm)

The love of Christ is beautiful, and that beautiful love came in the form of a normal and ordinary man. The great mystery which the Gospels proclaim is that in Jesus, God became flesh. He was born in obscurity and great humility, laid in a manger with the company of shepherds and livestock, and He looked so fragile. The prophet Isaiah describes the body of Christ as plain and unextraordinary. Jesus' physical body was not an Adonis-like figure. He was like one of us. Yet His love is far more beautiful than anything we could ever imagine, and now the great mystery is that He, in His infinite wisdom, has called His followers His body. Today, the church represents the physical body of Christ and his presence in the world. Certainly, we can say plenty about the ugliness of the church, but if Christ now calls the church his body, we should instead change our words to appreciation, awe, and gratitude that God has made something beautiful in the world in our shared company.

Closing Prayer

Jesus,

You truly are beautiful in every way. Beauty itself finds a definition in who You are as its creator. And what a beautiful thing You have created in calling us to be part of Your body in some great mystery of affection You have for Your followers. Teach us to see beauty in You, Your church, and the one You have called us to love.

Amen.

Our Relationship is Beautiful

Opening Prayer

Jesus,

We thank you for the beauty of your Word and the wisdom it has for us today. Please open our ears to hear you, our eyes to see your beauty, our hearts to receive your love, and our hands to be of service to you.

Amen.

Texts To Read

Song of Songs 1:1, 7:10

Matthew 18:20

Main Takeaway (Melody)

The Bible uses the phrase "the *blank* of *blank*" repeatedly. It is a Hebrew expression to display that the "*blank*" is the best "*blank*" to ever be. Therefore, we need to recognize that this song, the "Song of Songs," is claiming to be the greatest song ever written. There is no better song! It should be striking to us that the best song ever is a love song. It is a love song that displays an intense unity and physical intimacy between a husband and wife.

This intimacy is beautiful.

From the songwriter's perspective, there is no topic that is more beautiful. If there were, this would not be the best song ever! God designed our marital relationship, and the many factors of intimacy within it, as a beautiful gift. Sometimes our relationship does not seem to look or feel beautiful. Sometimes a marriage can seem routine, hurried, or frustrating. But God's design for marital intimacy and connection is to be a beautiful gift. When feelings of frustration or complacency arise, let us remember the beautiful gift that it is.

Challenge (Harmony)

In your own words, describe what makes your relationship beautiful with your spouse.

Look to Christ (Rhythm)

When was the last time you had a particular moment where you *felt* especially close to Jesus? Our faith should not be based on our feelings, but God gave us feelings for a reason. God gives us specific moments where we can feel a sense of intimacy with Christ, where we can be assured that He is with us, and those moments are a taste of what life will be like in the New Heaven and the New Earth. Just like you have moments where you may feel especially close to your spouse, God gives us moments where we can feel especially close to Him. Jesus promises us that when we gather in His name, for His glory, He promises to be there with us. Our faith will not feel that intimate every day, at least not in this life. But those moments are something to keep close to our heart and recognize as beautiful.

Closing Prayer

Jesus,

Thank You for always being with us. You promise to be here with us in all things, and we can be sure that is a guarantee because You are trustworthy. It is a beautiful and intimate matter to know that we can count on You being there for us. In the same way, teach us to do the same with our spouse. Teach us to find our relationship beautiful, and guide us to nurture that relationship into deeper beauty.

Amen.

Our Innate Worth is Beautiful

Opening Prayer

Jesus,

We thank you for the beauty of your Word and the wisdom it has for us today. Please open our ears to hear you, our eyes to see your beauty, our hearts to receive your love, and our hands to be of service to you.

Amen.

Texts To Read

Song of Songs 1:6-9

Ephesians 2:1-10

Main Takeaway (Melody)

The bride did not see her own physical beauty before falling in love, and she questioned how the groom could love her because she did not see herself as attractive. On the other hand, the groom saw her worth and beauty and desired for his bride to see herself as he did. Why? Because her beauty captivated his heart. While the bride does not see her own beauty, the groom finds her worthy of being adorned with exquisite jewelry.

We must never forget the worth of our spouse and our responsibility to help them see themselves as beautiful as we see them.

Why? Because they are worth being treated this way. How we treat our spouse is a direct reflection of how we see their worth. A person's self-worth is often directly related to how they have been treated. If we treat our spouse poorly, they will think little of themselves. But if we treat our spouse with great worth, honor, respect, and love, our spouse will see their worth and beauty in time for themselves.

Challenge (Harmony)

Share with your partner what you most appreciate about them right now

Look to Christ (Rhythm)

God made us with a deep beauty that goes beyond mere physicality. By our sin and rebellion, we lost our initial and God-given beauty as perfect beings with a God-given vocation, but that does not mean we lost our worth. Despite our sin God still loved us and saw us as having innate worth. God actively sought to rescue us, free us, and restore us by His grace and mercy. His intention was to restore us to be something beautiful, a bride for Jesus. The Church is His bride, made up of redeemed believers that Jesus died for. Christ has given us worth and poured out His immeasurable riches of grace and kindness on His beautiful bride.

Closing Prayer

Jesus,

Thank You that You see us for who we really are, not in how we might perceive ourselves. Thank you that You pursue us, seek after us, and want to see us restored. Thank You that our ultimate worth is found in You. Help us take these thanksgivings and bring them into our most intimate and vital relationships.

Amen.

Free Book

Thank you for reading our Song of Songs devotional!

We hope it brought a deeper appreciation for God's Word and you found it refreshing to your soul. To show our appreciation for you reading this devotional, we would like to offer you another one for free.

You can get a free copy of our book, *A Leader's Heart: A 31 Day Devotional Through The Letters of 1 and 2 Timothy*, by joining our mailing list at www.archippushouse.com[1].

We would ask that if you enjoyed this book that you would consider leaving a review online wherever you purchased it from. Your review means everything to us, as it helps give this book more exposure.

And if you found this devotional uplifting, the highest honor you can give us would be to share it with a friend to encourage them.

Again, thanks for reading this short devotional of ours.

Sincerely,

Mason D. Powell and Alexander Hildebrand

---

1. http://www.archippushouse.com

About the Authors

Alexander Hildebrand

Alexander Hildebrand is a pastor, author, musician, and amateur coffee roaster. He lives in Altoona, PA with his wonderful wife Emily and their three daughters, Genevieve, Zoeyanna, and Felicity. He is the co-author of *Rhythm of Love* and author of *The Promise and the Kingdom catechism*. He is currently serving as a pastor at First Church of Christ in Altoona, and writes/produces music with the band Valtune.

Mason D. Powell

Mason is the Teaching Co-Pastor at The Bluff Church in Poplar Bluff, MO. You can check out his messages by going to www.thebluff.church. Mason also writes fiction under the name of Mason Dakota. You can find all of Mason's books at www.booksbymason.com[1]. Mason is happily married to his wife, Jodi, and together they enjoy teaching their daughter, Harper, and son, Micah, to love God and love people.

All glory be to Christ our King.

---

1. http://www.booksbymason.com

Did you love *Rhythm of Love*? Then you should read *He Came To Dwell: Seeing Jesus Interact With Our World*[2] by Mason D. Powell!

[3]

Have you ever wondered if Jesus can relate to your life?

He lived two thousand years ago, and since he was God, then surely you would think he couldn't relate to your struggles. Or so many tend to believe. We worship him as God, but do we really believe Jesus knows how we feel, knows what we are going through, knows what it is like to be us?

Here's the truth: Jesus knows what it is like to be you.

---

2. https://books2read.com/u/318zYn

3. https://books2read.com/u/318zYn

The Gospel of John powerfully shows us that Jesus desires to be part of our lives. Often we read the Gospels to see that Jesus is God, but rarely do we look at them to discover what it is like for God to walk a mile in our shoes.

In this book, Mason explores that concept by looking at the ways Jesus deals with:

Our social anxiety.Our insecurities and lonelinessOur personal desire for achievement and redemption.

In addition to these things, this book also looks at topics like:

Seeing Jesus deal with grief.Seeing Jesus handle broken relationships.Seeing Jesus help us find our purpose in life.

When we see that Jesus came to dwell with us, to know us and be known by us, we see the key to being all that God would have us to be.

Read more at www.booksbymason.com.

About the Publisher

Archippus is a ministry created by Mason D. Powell and Alexander Hildebrand that exists to encourage followers of Jesus to pursue the work God has called them to do. Why? Because Jesus calls us to follow him, and in our call to follow, we receive a call to work.

We want every follower of Christ to recognize that they have already received a call to do good work for the Kingdom of God. Our vision, and our name, comes out of Colossians 4:17, "And say to Archippus, "See that you fulfill the ministry that you have received in the Lord."

Because of this vision, we seek to help people feel validated in their unique calling and tasks, and to foster Gospel creativeness. We want to help people see the divine purpose behind what God has called them to. God has called everyone to some particular work, and it's good, so go do it!

In 2023, Mason and Alex launched the Archippus podcast where they, and guests, discuss the theology of work. The podcast records casual conversations on how the Bible presents us with a Christ-centered mission to do good work in the Kingdom of God. You can listen to the Archippus podcast on Apple Podcasts, Google Podcasts, Spotify, or wherever you like to listen to podcasts.

You can also check it out on our website, www.archippushouse.com, where you can also check out our other work and resources.

If you are curious to know more about Archippus, consider joining our mailing list by going to www.archippushouse.com. When you join our mailing list you will receive:

An exclusive bonus chapter from *He Came To Dwell: Seeing Jesus Interact With Our World. A Leader's Heart: A 31-Day Devotional Through The Letters Of 1 And 2 Timothy Rhythm of Exile*, a mailing list exclusive prayer guide developed by Mason and Alex.

From Mason and Alex over at Archippus, we thank you for reading this book and being a supporter of our mission to encourage followers of Jesus to pursue the work God has called them to do.

Read more at www.archippushouse.com.